A Beginner's Guide to Bemba

A Beginner's Guide to Bemba

Gostave C Kasonde and Joan Haig

The Lembani Trust
LUSAKA

http://sites.google.com/site/lembanitrust/

First published 2010 by the Lembani Trust
Lusaka, Zambia

Copyright © Lembani Trust 2010

All rights reserved. Except for brief quotations in a review, this book, or any part thereof, may not be reproduced, stored into or introduced into a retrieval system, or transmitted, in any form or by any means, electronic, mechanical, photocopying, recording, or otherwise, without the written permission of the copyright owner.

ISBN 978-9982-9972-2-5

Lembani Trust books are distributed worldwide by
the African Books Collective, Oxford.
www.africanbookscollective.com

A Beginner's Guide to Bemba

The purpose of this guide is to provide a structured set of lessons for those interested in learning Bemba. Following these lessons will give students of Bemba a basic level of understanding and conversation skills.

The best way to become conversant in a language is, of course, to practice speaking. Bemba-speaking Zambians will appreciate your efforts and help you along.

We would like to thank Hazel Powell,
Veronica Haig and Jan-Bart Gewald for
their help, and Jim Haig for his illustration work.

Ishuko—Good luck!

Gostave Kasonde and Joan Haig

A note on pronunciation and spelling:

Although Bemba is for the most part phonetic, there are a few important points to note about pronunciation of words. There are also various ways of expressing pronunciation in written Bemba, so words in this guide may vary slightly in spelling from others.

The letter 'c' is always pronounced 'tch' (as in 'catch')
A = ah (as in 'father')
E = e (as in 'bed')
I = ee (as in 'bee')
O = (as in 'box')
U = oo (as in 'put')

There is no v, r, q, z or x in the Bemba alphabet. Words in Bemba do not begin with 'h'; when 'h' is at the end of a word it is usually succeeded by a vowel. The letter 'j' is usually preceded by 'n', to form 'ŋ' (as in 'swing').

Bemba is a tone language – this means that words spoken with different tone patterns can mean different things. This is not reflected in the spelling nor in this book. Listen carefully to the tone in the pronunciation of Bemba speakers and try to copy it.

A note of the layout of the book:

The lessons are in order of topics that emerged in our classes together, rather than following any comprehensive language learning formula. Each exercise builds on the one before it, so we recommend that you follow lessons in order. Check your answers with the lessons and with Bemba speakers.

Bemba words are printed in bold
Responses in Bemba are in italics

Information boxes contain key words or explanations.

Some lessons will include verb tables. However, not all the verb tenses are conjugated here.

8

CONTENTS

LESSON ONE	Greetings, key words, and words relating to money	11
LESSON TWO	**Ukuya**, to go, **ukutandala**, to visit and **ncito**, work	15
LESSON THREE	Exchanging names, transport, **ukwikala**, to stay, **ukwisa**, to come, and **langa**, to show	19
LESSON FOUR	Family relations, introducing others, enquiring after other people's family	23
LESSON FIVE	**Ukupeela**, to give, vocabulary building, and turning statements into questions	27
LESSON SIX	Numbers, linking vowels	31
LESSON SEVEN	Words with letter 'i', and days, weeks and months	35
LESSON EIGHT	**Ukulya**, to eat, vocabulary-building, and questions and phrases related to food	39
LESSON NINE	Parts of the body and some useful ways of describing people	45
LESSON TEN	Some more verbs as questions, and some useful negatives	51
GLOSSARY	List of some verb infinitives, and some further reading	55

LESSON ONE

We begin by learning some common greetings and formalities. In this lesson we also learn some questions, key words, and words relating to money.

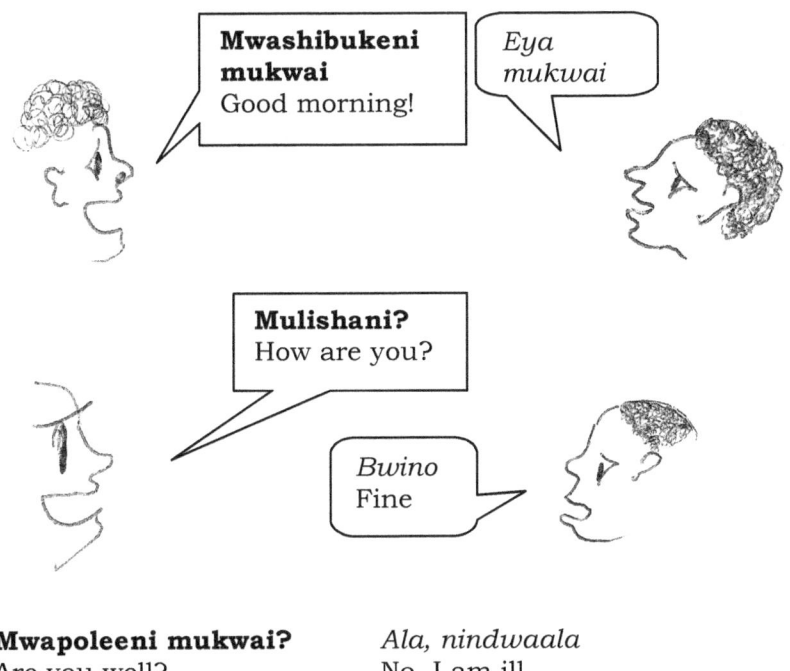

Mwashibukeni mukwai
Good morning!

Eya mukwai

Mulishani?
How are you?

Bwino
Fine

Mwapoleeni mukwai?   *Ala, nindwaala*
Are you well?   No, I am ill

MUKWAI is a polite address towards others.
EYA MUKWAI or **ENDITA MUKWAI** are polite ways of saying 'yes' or 'thank you' in response to a greeting.
AWE or **ALA** means 'no'.

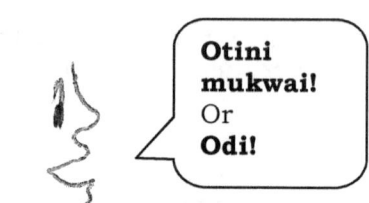

Otini mukwai! Or **Odi!**

Kalibu! Welcome! Or *Nalaisa mukwai!* I'm coming!

'Karibu' is a Swahili word for 'welcome'. It is widely used by Bemba speakers but prounounced **'Kalibu'**.

Mwashibukeni
Good morning/how did you wake?

Mwabombeni
Greetings (To somebody at work)

Mwalileni
Greetings (To somebody resting or eating)

Mwaikalenipo mukwai
Greetings (When you arrive at a host's house)

Mwatandalenipo mukwai?
Greetings (When you greet a guest in your house)

Ifintu filibwino?
How are things?

Shaleenipo
Goodbye

Tukamonana mailo
See you tomorrow

Twalamonana
See you later

Mwende bwino!
Safe journey!

Questions and Key Words

Naani?	Who?
Cinshi?	What, why?
Kwi?	Where?
Cisa?	Which?
Shani?	How?
Nishinga?	How much?
Linga?	How often?

Below is a list of key words, some of which stand alone and some of which are useful linking words. Try to memorise these if you can. Use this as a reference list for making sentences later in the book.

Apa/kuno = here
Apo = there
Iseni kuno = come here

Ici = this
Ico = that
Cinshi ico? = What's that?
Finshi ifyo? = What are those?

Cine cine = certainly, surely, at least
Cimo cine = same thing
Capwa = it's finished, it's empty
Panono = at least, slowly, a little
Fyapwa = finished (things)

Pa = at, on
Na = and, also, by, with
Ku = to
Kuli = for (place)
Mu = in
Pantu = because
Nalimo = maybe
Libili = often
Pe na pe = always

EXERCISES

Fill in the responses:

1. Mwashibukeni, mukwai ....
2. Mulishani? ....
3. Mwabombeni, mukwai ....
4. Otini mukwai! ....
5. Mwaikalenipo mukwai ....

Translate the following out loud:

1. Good morning!
2. Thank you. How are you?
3. Where?
4. Greetings (to somebody at work)
5. How much?
6. I'm coming!
7. See you later.
8. What's that?
9. Greetings (to your host)
10. How are things?

LESSON TWO

In this lesson we tackle the verb **ukuya**, to go. We will construct questions and responses using this verb and **ukutandala**, to visit, and **ncito**, to work.

UKUYA: TO GO

Present Continuous Tense

Naya	I am going
Waya	You are going
Aya	S/he is going
Twaya	We are going
Mwaya	You (plural/respect) are going
Baya	S/he (formal) is going
Baya	They are going

Past Tense

Naile	I went
Waile	You went
Aile	S/he went
Twaile	We went
Baile	S/he (plural/respect) went
Baile	They went

Near Future Tense (if going immediately or very soon)

Nalaya	I will go
Uleya	You will go
Aleya/alaya	S/he will go
Tuleya	We will go
Muleya	You (plural/respect) will go
Baleya	They will go

Future Tense (if going later in day or in future)

Nkaya	I will go
Ukaya	You will go
Akaya	S/he will go
Tukaya	We will go
Bakaya	They will go
Mukaya	You (formal/plural) will go

Question:	**Ba Susan mwaile kwi?**
	Susan, where did you go?
Answer:	*Naile ku Mbala*
	I went to Mbala
Question:	**Finshi mwaile mukucita?**
	What did you go to do?
Answer:	*Naile mukutandala*
	I went for a visit
Question:	**Ba Susan, mwaile ku Mpulungu—finshi mwaile mukucita?**
	Susan, you went to Mpulungu—what did you go to do?
Answer:	*Naile kuncito*
	I went for work

MAILO means both 'yesterday' and 'tomorrow'. The verb indicates which is meant. For example, Susan is going to Mbala tomorrow and Tom went yesterday.

Susan:	**Mailo nkaya ku Mbala**
Tom:	*Ah! Mailo naile ku Mbala*

UKUTANDALA is the verb 'to visit'. **TANDALA** is the noun, 'visit'.
Naile mukutandala
I went to/for a visit

FINSHI means 'what?'

There are two meanings for the word **LIMBI**. It can be used to say 'later' or 'another time'. It can also be used to place doubt on a statement.
Mwise limbi
Come later
Tukamonana mailo limbi
Maybe I will see you tomorrow

EXERCISES

Translate the following:

1. Mailo waile kwi James?

   ....

2. Mailo ukaya ku England?

   ....

3. Mailo mwaile ku cinsankano

   ....

4. Maybe I will see you tomorrow

   ....

5. What did you go to do in Lusaka?

   ....

6. Yesterday I went to Livingstone

   ....

7. I went for a visit

   ....

8. Come later for a visit!

   ....

LESSON THREE

Here we will learn how to exchange names, and where we come from. We also learn some words relating to transport, and common ways to use the verbs **ukwikala**, to stay, **ukwisa**, to come, and **langa**, to show.

VOCABULARY

Ishina	Name
Ituka	Shop
Amatuka	Shops
Icimbusu	Toilet
Cisankano	Market
Sacha	Bus
Indeke	Aeroplane
Pakapaka	Helicopter
Icibansa ca ndeke	Airport

Did you know? The word for helicopter comes from the sound of the rotors.

Did you know? The word 'sacha' comes from the colonial bus company, which was named Thatcher and Hobson.

Ishina lyenu nimwe bani?
What is your name?

Ishina lyandi nine Patrick
My name is Patrick

UKWIKALA: TO STAY

Question: **Ba Patrick, mwikalakwi?**
Patrick, where do you stay?
Answer: *Njikala ku Kasama*
I stay in Kasama

UKWISA: TO COME

Question:	**Bushe ba Tom baliisa?**
	Did Tom come back?
Answer:	*Ba Tom tabaishile*
	Tom did not come back
Answer:	*Ba Tom tabalaisa*
	Tom has not come back (yet)

LANGA: TO SHOW

Nangeniko inshila yaku maliketi/cisankano
Show me the way to the market

Mulangeniko, show him/her
Tulangeniko, show us
Balangeniko, show them

Nangeniko ukuli icimbusu
Show me to the toilet

Bushe sacha ilikwi?
Where is the bus?

Bushe sacha ileya kwi?
Where is the bus going?

Sacha ileya ku Lusaka
The bus is going to Lusaka

Bushe waya kwi?
Where are you going?

Naya kwituka
I'm going to the shop

Note that often when a word ending with 'u' meets a word beginning with 'i' the two are joined by a 'w'
Above, **'ku'** meets **'ituka'** to become **'kwituka'**

EXERCISES

Translate the following:

1. Did Mark come by helicopter?

   ....

2. Yes, Mark came by helicopter

   ....

3. Nangeniko inshila yaku cibansa ca ndeke

   ....

4. Where is the road to the market?

   ....

5. Show them the bus going to Ndola

   ....

6. Bushe sacha yaku Harare naiisa?

   ....

7. Pakapaka aleya ku Ndola

   ....

8. Sacha aleya ku cisankano

   ....

LESSON FOUR

In this lesson we learn about our relations and how to address and introduce others, as well as asking after other people's families.

Nkashi (yandi)
(My) sister

Ndume (yandi)
(My) brother

> Use **nandi** if addressing own brother/sister when same sex

Umwaice (wandi)
(My) younger brother/sister

Umufyala (wandi)
(My) cousin

Umwana (wandi) umwaume
(My) son

Umwana (wandi) umwanakashi
(My) daughter

Umunandi
My friend

Abafyashi benu balishani?
How are your parents?

Balifye bwino
They are fine

> **Uyu** means 'this'. Use it when introducing people.

Uyu mukashi wandi
This is my wife

Uyu mulume wandi
This is my husband

Uyu munandi
This is my friend

Uyu mufyala wandi
This is my cousin

> Cousinship in Bemba is the relationship between the children of a brother and the children of his sister.

Uyu ni munyinane
This is my brother/sister

Aba ni bayama
This is my uncle (the brother to my mother)

Aba ni batata mwaice
This is my father's younger brother

Aba ni bamayo mwaice
This is my mother's sister

Aba ni bamayo senge
This is my aunt (sister to my father)

Aba ni bamayo mukalamba
This is my aunt (elder sister of my mother)

> **Muntu** is the Bemba word for a person. The shortened version of the word is derogatory and must be avoided.
> **Muntu wandi** means 'my relative'
> **Muntu onse** means 'anybody' or 'everybody'
> **Muntu** can also mean 'somebody', for example:
> **muntu anjebele** = somebody told me

EXERCISES

Fill in the gaps or translate:

LESSON FIVE

In this lesson we learn the basics of the verb **ukupeela**, to give. We will construct some sentences using the vocabulary in the box. We also look at the way in which statements can be turned into questions by the use of tone.

UKUPEELA/PEELA: TO GIVE

Present Tense

Napeela	I give
Wapeela	You give
Apeela	S/he gives
Twapeela	We give
Bapeela	They give

Interrogative/Recent Past Tense

Mpeele?	(Do) I give?	I have given
Wapeele? (plural, formal) **Upeele?** (singular)	You give?	You have given
Apeele?	S/he gives?	S/he has given
Tupeele?	We give?	We have given
Bapeele?	They give?	They have given

The above table shows two uses of this verb conjugation. The first is a question that can be used as a command. For example, you can ask the question, **Napeele ba Tom?** This means, Do (can, should, will) I give it to Tom?
OR you can command somebody, **Wapeele ba Tom?**
This means, Can (will) you give it to Tom?

The second use is straightforward recent past tense.

Mpeleeni	Give me
Mupeleeni	Give him/her
Tupeleeni	Give us
Bapeleeni	Give them
Bapeleeni	Give him/her (formal)

Statements and Questions

You can turn a statement into a question, or a question into a statement, by the tone of your voice.

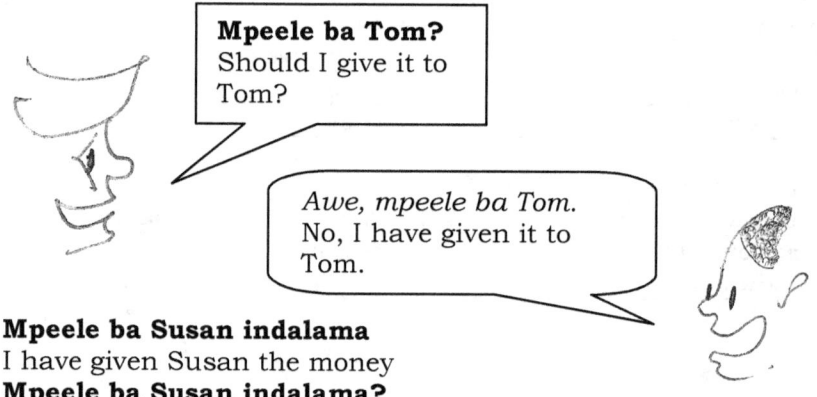

Mpeele ba Susan indalama
I have given Susan the money
Mpeele ba Susan indalama?
(Can) I give Susan the money?

Ndeya ku cisankano
I will go to the market
Ndeya ku cisankano?
Will (can) I go to the market?

Ukaya ku Nairobi
You will go to Nairobi.
Ukaya ku Nairobi?
Will you go to Nairobi?

EXERCISES

Make sentences using the words given, and practice saying them out loud.

1. **BAMAYO, LUSAKA**
....

2. **NKASHI, PAKA PAKA**
....

3. **UMUFYALA, ITUKA**
....

4. **BATATA, SPAIN**
....

5. **UMWIPWA, WABATATA**
....

6. **INSHILA, LIVINGSTONE**
....

7. **MAILO, MBALA**
....

8. **PAKAPAKA, LONDON**
....

9. **BUSHE, SCOTLAND**
....

10. **BAMAYO, CINSANKANO**?
....

Translate the following sentences:

1. Can I give Marian the money?

2. Is my uncle going to Cairo?

3. **Naya ku cibansa ca ndeke.**

4. **Pakapaka ali pa cibansa ca ndeke.**

5. My aunt will come.

6. My cousin stays in Germany.

7. Show me the way to the bus.

8. I will go by car.

9. **Nkaya mailo?**

10. **Mailo naile ku Mbala.**

Fill in the missing words:

Past	Present	Future
Naliiya	**Naya**	
		Bakaya
	Twaya	
Aliya		
		Mukaya
	Napeela	
	Namona	
	Leelo	

LESSON SIX

Here we learn the numbers in Bemba, from 1 to 10. We learn how to apply numbers to people, and practice constructing sentences involving numbers. In general, for numbers above 10, use English. We will also learn about linking words that end and begin with vowels.

		ROOT
ONE	**CIMO**	--MO
TWO	**FIBILI**	--BILI
THREE	**FITATU**	--TATU
FOUR	**FINE**	--NE
FIVE	**FISANO**	--SANO
SIX	**MUTANDA**	
SEVEN	**CINE LUBALI**	
EIGHT	**CINE KONSEKONSE**	
NINE	**PABULA**	
TEN	**IKUMI**	
20	**MAKUMI YABILI**	
100	**MWANDA UMO**	

		Prefix
PERSON	**UMUNTU**	**u-**
PEOPLE	**ABANTU**	**ba-**
CHILDREN	**ABANA**	**ba-**
YOUTH	**ABAICE**	**ba-**
MEN	**ABAUME**	**ba-**
WOMEN	**ABANAKASHI** or **BANAMAYO**	**ba-**
ELDERLY PERSON	**UMUKOTE**	**u-**
ELDERLY PEOPLE	**ABAKOTE**	**ba-**

The numbers 1-5 are CARDINAL numbers. They are adjectives that require a prefix. The prefix will change depending on the noun being used. Here, we learn how to apply numbers to people. Put the noun before the number.

When applying the number 1 to a person, use the root of the word (-**mo**) with the appropriate prefix (**u**-).
For example,
one person = **umuntu umo**

When applying the numbers 2-5 to people, use the root of the number with the appropriate prefix.
For example,
two people = **abantu babili**
three children = **abana batatu**

For 6 and above, use the full words with no prefix.
For example,
seven women = **banamayo cine lubali**
ten children = **abana ikumi**

EXERCISES

Construct sentences out loud using the following words:

1. **ITUKA, UMO, AKAYA**

2. **BASANO, LUSAKA, MOTOKA** (CAR)

3. **ABANA, INDEKE, MAILO, BANE**

4. **CINE KONSEKONSE, INDEKE, ICIBANSA CA NDEKE**

5. **BATATU, LONDON, NA, INDEKE**

6. **BAMAYO SENGE, BEKALA, BABILI, AMERICA**

7. **BASANO, ICISANKANO, ABAICE**

8. **CINE LUBALI, AMATUKA, ABAFYALA**

9. **MUTANDA, INSHILA, ABANTU**

10. **BANE, ABAICE, ITUKA**

Sometimes, when a word ending in 'a' is followed by a word beginning with 'i', the words are linked by dropping these letters and using 'e'. For example, **na indeke** becomes **nendeke**.

Sometimes, when a word ending in 'u' meets a word beginning with 'i', the words are linked by dropping the 'u' and replacing with 'w'. For example, **ku ituka** becomes **kwituka**. (This does not apply to **icibansa ca ndeke**.)

LESSON SEVEN

Now we are going to construct some sentences and learn about words that begin with the letter 'i'. We will also learn about days, weeks and months.

Nouns beginning with the letter 'i' are treated differently from other words. Verbs and adjectives relating to them take on the prefix **i-** and **y-** if singular and **sha-** and **shi-** if plural.

For example:

If there is only one aeroplane, the correct sentence would be, **Indeke imo yalaya ku cibansa ca ndeke**.

If were three aeroplanes, the correct sentence would be, **Indeke shitatu shalaya ku cibansa ca ndeke**.

If nine aeroplanes will go to the airport, the correct sentence would be, **Indeke pabula shalaya ku cibansa ca ndeke**.

Now try making sentences out loud with the following words:

IMBWA Dog/s

INDEKE Aeroplane/s

INAMA Animal/s (also meat)

IMBALE Plate/s

INSAPATO Shoes

Days, Weeks, Months

Monday	**Pali cimo**
Tuesday	**Pali cibili**
Wednesday	**Pali citatu**
Thursday	**Pali cine**
Friday	**Pali cisano**
Saturday	**Pa cibelushi**
Sunday ("Day of God")	**Pa nshiku ya mulungu**
Week	**Umulungu**
Month/moon	**Umweshi**
Year	**Umwaka**
One day	**Ubushikubumo**
Days	**Inshiku**
Night-time	**Ubushiku**
Daytime/sun	**Akasuba**
Evening	**Icungulo**
One week	**Umulungu umo**
Two weeks	**Imilungu ibili**
Three weeks	**Imilungu itatu**
... Six weeks	**Imilungu mutanda**
This week	**Uyumulungu**
Next week	**Uyumulungu uleisa**
Last week	**Uyumulungu wapwile**
This month	**Uno mweshi**
Next month	**Uyu mweshi uleisa**
Last month	**Uyu mweshi wapwile**
This year	**Uno mwaka**
Next year	**Uyu mwaka uleisa**
Last year	**Uyu mwaka wapwile/ Uwafumineko**

EXERCISES

Make sentences out loud using the following words:

1. **PALI CIBILI, INDEKE, IMO, LONDON**

2. **PA CITATU, MPULUNGU, UYUMULUNGU**

3. **UYUMWESHI, INDEKE, SCOTLAND**

4. **PALICISANO, ICISANKANO, UMUFYALA WANDI**

5. **IMBWA, IN'GANDA, SHINE, PALI CIMO**

6. **CIBELUSHI, ICISANKANO, BAMAYO**

7. **PA NSHIKU YA MULUNGU, GERMANY, INDEKE**

Construct a short story:

....

....

....

....

....

....

....

LESSON EIGHT

In this lesson we learn about food and practice some basic phrases related to eating.

UKULYA: TO EAT

Ndeelya	I am eating
Uleelya	You are eating (informal)
Aleelya	S/he is eating
Tuleelya	We are eating
Baleelya	They are eating (plural/formal)

food = **ifyakulya**
water = **ameenshi**
milk = **umukaka**
tea = **tii**
coffee = **kofi**
sugar = **shuka/insukale**
salt = **umucele**
chilli = **impilipili**
gravy = **umuuto**

egg = **ilini**
eggs = **amaani**

relish = **umunani**
meat = **inama**
beef = **n'gombe**
lamb = **impaanga**
goat = **imbushi**
pork = **inkumba**
chicken = **inkoko**

vegetables = **umusalu**
beans = **cilemba**
tomato = **matimati**
onion = **kanyanse**
cabbage = **kabeji**
rape = **rape**
pumpkin leaves = **cibwabwa**
potato = **ifyumbu**
sweet potato = **kandolo**
Irish potato = **ifilashi/ imbatata**
nshima (mealie meal) = **ubwali**
cassava = **kalundwe/tuute**
maize = **amataba**
rice = **umupunga**

Relish is the dish, usually meat or beans, that accompanies nshima

Umfwile is the verb 'to hear'. **Nsala** means 'hunger'.
Naumfwa nsala literally means, 'I hear hunger'.

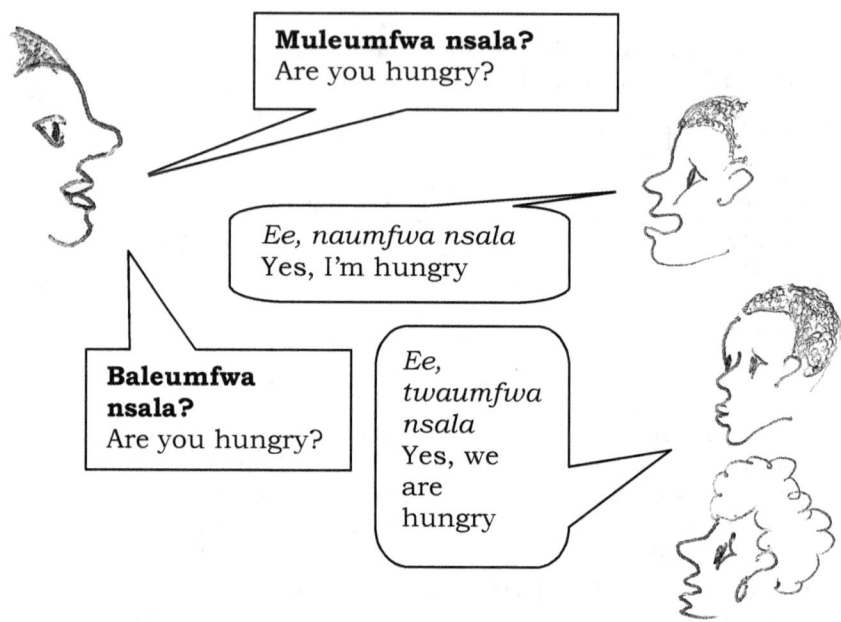

I want	**Ndefwaya**
You want	**Ulefwaya**
S/he wants	**Alefwaya**
We want	**Tulefwaya**
They want	**Balefwaya**
You (formal, plural) want	**Mulefwaya**

Musalu nshi mukwete?
What vegetables do you have?

Tukwete cabbage na cibwabwa...
We have cabbage and pumpkin leaves...

I have	**Ninkwata**
You have	**Naukwata**
S/he has	**Nakwata**
We have	**Natukwata**
They have	**Nabakwata**
You (formal, plural) have	**Namukwata**

Namukwata umunani?
Do you have relish?
OR
Munani nshi mukwete?
What relish do you have?

Tukwete ngombe, isabi...
We have beef, fish...

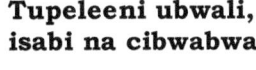

Tupeleeni ubwali, isabi na cibwabwa

Give us nshima, fish and pumpkin leaves

UKUSALUULA is 'to fry'
Fried egg = **amaani ayasalulwa**
Fried fish = **isabi iyasalulwa**

UKWIPIKA (or **IPIKA**) is 'to cook', 'to boil'
Boiled fish = **isabi iyaipikwa**

UKUKANGA (or **KANGA**) is 'to roast'
Roasted meat = **inama iyakukanga**

Amenshi yaku<u>nwa</u>
Drinking water

UKUNWA means 'to drink'

Amenshi yaku samba
Water to wash

UKUSAMBA means 'to wash' the body or part of the body
(**UKUCHAPA** means 'to wash' clothes or things)

Mpeleeniko amenshi
Pass me/give me water

Mpeleeniko amenshi yakusamba kuminwe
Give me water to wash my hands

Iminwe = fingers

Mpeleeniko isabi na limbi?
Can I have more fish?

Mpeleeniko ilini na limbi
Or **Mpeleeniko amani na yambi**
Give me another egg

Mpeleeniko ubwali na bwumbi
Pass me more nshima

Note the different ways that you can use the verb **ukupeela,** to give.

Na limbi means 'again' or 'a second time'. Note how the form of this changes depending on the starting vowel of the noun in use – for example, **yambi** and **bumbi**.

Naikuta!
I'm full up!

EXERCISES

Make sentences out loud with the following words:

1. **BABILI, ABAICE, ITUKA**

2. **MUTANDA, BANAMAYO, ICISANKANO**

3. **CINE LUBALI, ABAUME, IN'GANDA** (HOUSE)

4. **BASANO, AMUNTU, AMATUKA**

5. **PABULA, INDEKE, ICIBANSA CA NDEKE**

Translate the following:

1. Give me some water

2. I'm hungry

3. I want fried fish

4. This is my sister. She wants nshima

5. What relish do you have?

6. What is your name?

7. Are you hungry?

8. Pass me some sugar

9. Show me the way to the market

10. Give me six eggs

LESSON NINE

In this lesson we learn about the parts of the body, some Bemba sayings that relate to the body, and some ways to describe people.

skin
inkanda

head
umutwe

face
icinso

neck
umukoshi

shoulder/s
icipeya/amapeya
OR **ukwapa**

chest/breasts
icifuba/amabeele

arm/arms
ukuboko/amaboko

elbow
nkonkoni

stomach
ifumo

waist
umusana

hip
intungu

thigh/thighs
itaanta/amataanta
leg
umukonso/amukonso
knee/knees
ikuufi/amakuufi

foot/feet
ulukasa/amakasa
toe/toes
ifikondo/akakondo

eye/eyes
ilinso/amenso

nose/noses
**umoona/
imyona**

mouth
akanwa

lips
imilomo

chin
kalefulefu

hair
umushishi

ear/ears
kutwi/amatwi

---

hand
icisansa

finger/fingers
iminwe/umunwe

thumb
icikumo

wrist
nkolokoso

> There are many words for 'hair', depending on to where it grows on the body:
> Hair on the head	**imishishi/umushishi**
> Leg or arm hair	**ubupipi**
> Beard/moustache	**imyefu**
> Armpits	**umushishi wamukwapa**

UKABA TO BE

I am	Ndi
You are	Uli
He/She is	Ali
We are	Tuli
They are	Bali
You are (plural, formal)	Muli

Someone who lies or gossips
Alikwata umulomo
(**imilomo** = lips)

A philanderer
Alikwata ulwinso
(**amenso** = eyes)

Someone who likes talking
Alikwata akanwa
(**akanwa** = mouth)

Secret police or CID
Bamatwimatwi
(**amatwi** = ears)

Language
Ululimi
(**Ululimi** = tongue)

Claire is expecting a baby
Claire akwata ifumo
(**ifumo** = stomach)

As you know, there are many ways to describe people. Here we learn to describe people by where they are from and the ways they look.

Europeans	**abasungu**
Black Africans	**abafita**
Arabs	**abalungwana**
Indians/South Asians	a**bamwenye**
Afrikaners	**amabunu**

handsome
beautiful
= **ubusuma**

ugly/shabby/bad
= **ubuubi**

tall
umutali

short
umwipi

fat
uwaina

thin
uwaonda

young
umwaice

old
umukote

EXERCISES:

Translate the following:

1. This is my friend. She is a gossip!

2. My name is Bwalya. What is your name? Where do you come from? I come from Ndola.

3. I have one sister. She is expecting a baby.

4. My mother is short but my father is tall.

5. Good morning. Where is the bus to Kitwe?

6. This is Susan. We are going to England next week.

7. Tomorrow you will go to the shops

8. He is handsome!

9. Last week I went to Lake Tanganyika with my husband.

10. The dog is fat!

Name the different parts of the body:

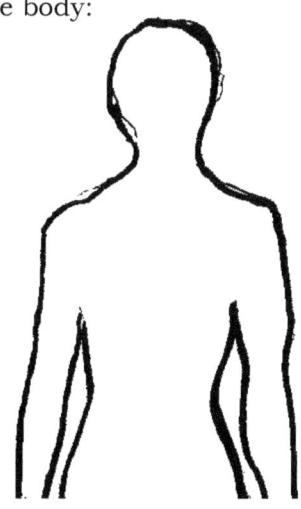

LESSON TEN

This final lesson will introduce some more verbs as questions, and also teach some negatives.

I know
Ninjishiba

I don't know
Nshishibe

Do you know?
Nawishiba?

You don't know?
Tawishibe?

I think so
Natontonkanya ati
I don't think so
Awe tefyo ndetontonkanya

What do you think?
Uletontonkanya shani?
You don't think so?
Tenfyo uletontonkanya?

I want
Ndefwaya

I don't want
Shilefwaya

You don't want	**Taulefwaya**
S/he doesn't want	**Talefwaya**
We don't want	**Tatulefwaya**
They don't want	**Tabalefwaya**

Go!
Kabiye!

Don't go!
Wiiya!

Are you going?
Uleeya?

You are not going
Tawaye

I like it
Nacitemwa

I don't like it
Nshicitemenwe

You don't like it	Taucitemenwe
S/he doesn't like it	Tacitemenwe
We don't like	Tatucitemenwe
They don't like it	Tabacitemenwe

I have (money)
Ninkwata (ndalama)

I don't have (money)
Shikwete (ndalama)

You don't have	Taukwete
S/he doesn't have	Takwete
We don't have	Tatukwete
They don't have	Tabakwete

I need that
Ndefwaya/nakabile ico

I don't need that
Nshilefwaya ico

Do you need that?
Ulefwaya ico?

You don't need that
Taulefwaya ico

I'm hungry
Ndine nsala

I'm not hungry
Nshikwete insala

I feel hungry
Naumfwa nsala

I don't feel hungry
Nshileeumfwa nsala

I feel well
Naumfwa bwino

I don't feel well
Nshileumfwa bwino

I am happy
Nitwemwa

I am not happy
Nshitemenwe

I am tired
Nanaka/ninaka

I am not tired
Nshinakile/nshilanaka

Do you speak Bemba?
Mulalanda iciBemba?

I speak Bemba
Ndalaanda iciBemba

I don't speak Bemba
Nshilanda ciBemba

I speak a little Bemba
Ndalanda iciBemba panono

I am learning Bemba
Nde sambilila iciBemba

EXERCISES

Make up questions and answers using negatives:

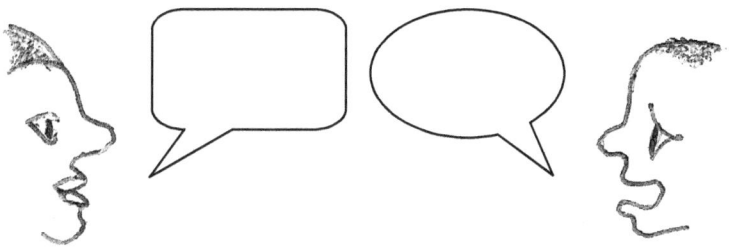

Translate the following out loud:

1. Where is the bus? Do you know? I don't know.

2. I don't feel well. Show me to the hospital (**cipataala**)

3. No, I don't want it and I don't have money!

4. Come here! I need my book (**citabo**)

5. You don't want it? What do you want?

Do you speak Bemba?
....
....
....

Yes, I speak a little Bemba
....
....
....

GLOSSARY

Some verb infinitives

To be	**ukaba**
To buy	**ukushita**
To come	**ukwisa**
To drink	**ukunwa**
To eat	**ukulya**
To give	**ukupeela**
To go	**ukuya**
To have	**ukukwata**
To show	**langa**
To speak	**ukulanda**
To stay	**ukwikala**
To visit	**ukutandala**
To want	**ukufwaya**
To work	**ncito**

Suggested reading

There are several useful books available for purchase, and we urge you to take a look at these to supplement your learning. These include:

Bemba Pocket Dictionary (1992)
Rev. E. Hoch, W.F. The Society of the Missionary for Africa

Zambian Phrase Book (2000)
Khozi, M. and Grant, H. Venus Stationary Ltd

An Outline of iciBemba Grammar (1999) [This is for advanced linguists.]
Mann, M. Bookworld Publishers

Icibemba Cakwa Chitimukulu (1982)
Oger, L. Chinsali Language Centre

www.ingramcontent.com/pod-product-compliance
Lightning Source LLC
Chambersburg PA
CBHW051530230426
43668CB00012B/1802